A MOMENT
IN RHYME

A MOMENT IN RHYME

COLIN WEST
AND JULIE BANYARD

Dial Books for Young Readers

New York

To Caroline Roberts
We dedicate truly
These poems and pictures,
Love Colin and Julie.

CONTENTS

THE SILENT SHIP

I sailed a ship as white as snow,
As soft as clouds on high,
Tall was the mast, broad was the beam,
And safe and warm was I.

I stood astern my stately ship
And felt so grand and high,
To see the lesser ships give way
As I went gliding by.

SILVER SLIPPERS

A legend says whoever tries
These silver slippers on for size,
And finds the silver slippers fit,
Will gallivant and dance and flit
Around the room, across the floor,
And past the sofa, through the door,
Into the garden, down the lane,
And never will be seen again.
Who wishes to perchance be gone?
Will no one try these slippers on?

MARKET SQUARE

I went to market with my pig,
My merry pig called Gus,
Proud stood we there in Market Square,
But no one noticed us.

Matthew sold his barleycorn,
And Edward sold his berries,
Nancy sold her seven hens,
And Sally sold her cherries.

Simon sold his ancient plough,
And Ann her father's gig,
Jenny sold her mother's pies,
Yet no one bought my pig.

But when the folk had homeward gone,
Beneath a moonlit sky,
Gay danced we there, in Market Square,
My merry pig and I.

CAROLINE IN COTTON RAGS

Here's Catherine in crinoline,
And Celia in silk,
And Claudia in dimity
With skin as white as milk.

And yet with all this finery,
This taffeta and lace,
It's Caroline in cotton rags
Who has the fairest face.

THE TREE AND THE SEASONS

Spring is a green
And gracious friend
Who fans me with
Her gentle wind.

Summer is a
Sultry lover
Who burns my heart
Until she's over.

Autumn is a
Cunning thief
Who robs me of
My every leaf.

Winter is a
Cruel master
Who chills me till
Sweet Spring comes after.

BOXES

(Can you match the picture with the verse?)

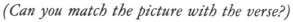

Turn the key,
A tinkling sound,
A tiny dancer
Twirls around.

Cylindrical,
With ribbon on it,
Inside you'll find
A pretty bonnet.

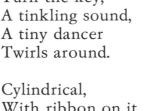

Through sun and storm
Within this box
Grow old man's beards
And lady's smocks.

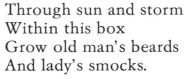

Lift the lid
And open wide –
Needles, pins
And threads inside.

A birthday gift
From boy to girl,
With coffee cream
And walnut whirl.

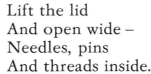
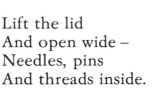

Locked inside
Are precious things –
Brooches, necklaces
And rings.

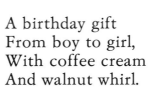

This box that's red
And rather grand
All year upon
The curb will stand.

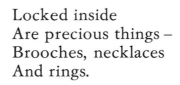

Lift the latch
And stand well back,
For out will jump
A boy called Jack.

12

THE VIOLIN-FIDDLE

The violin is highly strung
And melancholy is her song,
But should she choose to change her tune,
She'll fiddle 'neath a gypsy moon.

MY CAT

My cat can stalk,
My cat can prance,
My cat can skip,
My cat can dance.

My cat can yawn,
My cat can purr,
My cat can preen
His silky fur.

My cat can leap,
My cat can pounce,
My cat can bound,
My cat can bounce.

My cat can taunt,
My cat can tease,
My cat can hide
In boughs of trees.

My cat can plod,
My cat can prowl,
My cat can scratch,
My cat can growl.

My cat can do
Just anything,
But catch a bird
That's on the wing.

YOUNG BOY

Oh, I am just a young boy,
But when I'm fully grown,
Then I will be an Old Boy,
And Mayor of London Town.

I'll wear a chain of office
And robes all trimmed with fur,
And then my old schoolteachers
Will have to call *me* Sir.

THE FARMER'S SHADOW

Soft is the farmer's shadow
Upon the golden corn,
As we set off a-harvesting
In the early morn.

Swift is the farmer's shadow
When work is to be done.
The straw we bundle into sheaves
In the midday sun.

Long is the farmer's shadow
As we all make our way
Along the path that takes us home
At the end of day.

CLOUDS

Above me I see mountains,
The mountains of the sky,
They tumble down and spill about
So silently, till I
Can see them change to other things,
For now their shapes evoke
An avalanche of cotton wool
Or puffs of engine smoke.

And now here comes an ogre with
A club clenched in his fist;
His footsteps sound like thunder,
But he fades away to mist.
And now I see a mighty horse,
And now a flock of sheep,
And now I see the shepherd boy
A-lying down to sleep.

GOING TO THE BANK

When Uncle Ben goes to the bank,
I like to go there too,
But not for business purposes
As other people do.

I go to see the blotting pad
Which on the counter lies –
For there I know I'll find a treat
On which to feast my eyes.

For everything is back to front
In Blotting Paper Land –
Men's signatures and ladies' names
Writ in a magic hand!

Mere words become weird alphabets
Of dashes and of dots,
And who can guess what sorcery
Lies hidden in the blots?

And when I'm older, will *I* make
Strange marks on paper pink,
And leave behind *my* magic spell
In backward-slanting ink?

DAYS GONE BY

Who would I choose to be if I
Could have lived in days gone by?

Not a lady in a bower
Idly picking fruit or flower

Nor a cavalier's princess
In a flowing velvet dress

No, I would be a farmer's wife
And lead a plain and simple life.

CATCH IF YOU CAN

"Catch if you can, the moon from the sky,
The song of a blackbird,
The dance of the breeze on a field full of rye.
Then wrap them up in a gold buttercup
That floats upon the river
And I will love you ever."

I stretched for the moon, but could not reach,
The blackbird's song I could not sing,
The wheat and the wind wouldn't let me join in,
So alone now I float in my buttercup boat
Upon the silver river
That carries me forever.

A HAT

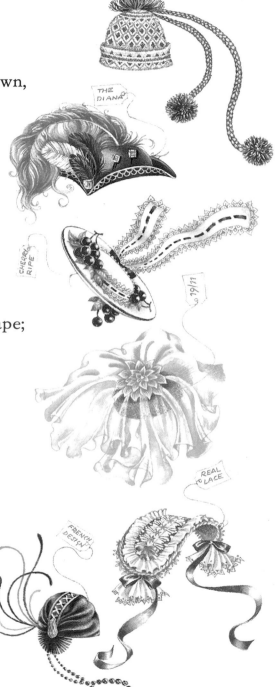

I'm going to the hatter
For to purchase me a hat.
It doesn't really matter
If it's tall or if it's flat.

I don't mind if it's black or brown,
Or if it has a crumpled crown,
Or if the brim is up or down;
A simple hat is all I ask,
To cover up my ears.

I don't ask for a bonnet
That is made of velveteen,
With a lot of ribbons on it
That are yellow, pink or green.

I don't ask for a hat of crêpe,
Or one of an exotic shape,
Or one that's all tied up with tape;
A simple hat is all I ask,
To cover up my ears.

I don't want one with feathers,
Or with cherries ripe and red,
A plain hat for all weathers
Would be fine for me instead.

I do not really mind a bit
If my hat's not a *perfect* fit,
If I can just get into it,
A simple hat is all I ask,
To cover up my ears.

THE THREE WISHES

If I had three wishes,
My first wish would be
To fly with the puffins
Who go out to sea.

If I had three wishes,
Then next I would wish
To lead with the pilchard
The life of a fish.

If I had three wishes,
I'd wish in the end
That puffin and pilchard
Were each other's friend.

MARY'S SENSES

On Monday Mary came to me
And held me to her eye;
I showed her stars and rainbows
Which were hidden in the sky.

On Tuesday Mary came to me
And held me to her ear;
And though we were far from the shore
The ocean she could hear.

On Wednesday Mary came to me
And held me to her nose;
When I'm in bloom my heavy head
With perfume overflows.

On Thursday Mary came to me
And held me to her lips;
For no fruit tastes as sweet as mine
Whose skin is strewn with pips.

On Friday Mary came to me
And held me to her cheek:
The softest and the lightest thing
Her skin has touched all week.

WILD FLOWERS

The thought of a fox
Ever putting on socks,
Is silly, my love,
Yet here's a foxglove.

Pray, tell me what flower
Can tell you the hour
Without a tick-tock?
A dandelion clock.

Now, what is it grows
Wherever one goes
Where sweethearts have kissed?
'Tis love-in-a-mist.

I read in a rhyme
Of flowers that chime;
This didn't ring true,
Yet bluebells seem to.

And only in tales
From China or Wales
Live dragons, perhaps,
Yet here's one who snaps.

RAINBOW SHIP

Two dreams I've always cherished:
To sail upon the main,
And to regard a rainbow
Without a drop of rain.

That rainbow seemed elusive,
I never sailed the sea,
Until Uncle Horatio
A present gave to me:

A Ship Inside a Bottle!
Now in its glassy realm,
My little ship goes sailing,
With me stood at the helm.

And when the sun is shining
Upon the glass, I've found,
Without a single raindrop,
A rainbow's all around.

HOME

I am a pebble
Shiny red,
My home is on
The river bed.

I am a silver
Paper clip,
My home is on
A memo slip.

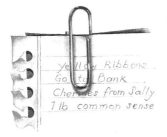

I am a yellow
Lollipop,
My home is in
The village shop.

I am a towel
With stripes of pink,
My home is by
The kitchen sink.

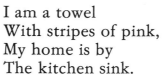

I am a golden
Twenty-four,
My home is on
An oaken door.

I am a kite
Of many hues,
My home is where
The wind should choose.

THE LADYBIRD TRAVELLER

You've heard of a Bee in the Bonnet,
You've heard of a Fly on the Wall,
Well, I am a Ladybird Traveller,
Who travels the world at a crawl.

Frontiers for me aren't a problem
I pass over mountains with ease,
I can stroll round the world in an hour
And cross all the Seven High Seas.

The Tropics, the Poles, the Equator,
I can visit them all in a day:
An afternoon spent in the Indies,
An evening spent in Cathay.

Africa, Asia and Europe,
My world is a peaceable place,
But should I one day find it tiresome,
I shall simply fly off into space.

COMMONSENSE

If Commonsense were sold in shops,
I'd purchase me a pound:

I'd give a quarter
To Sir John,

A quarter
To Miss Brown,

A quarter to
Old Algernon,

A quarter to
His hound.

And all the Commonsense left over,
I'd put it on the shelf,
Wrapped in a cotton handkerchief,
And keep it for myself.

THE FATHER CHRISTMAS ON THE CAKE

For fifty weeks I've languished
Upon the cupboard shelf,
Forgotten and uncared for,
I've muttered to myself.
But now the year is closing,
And Christmastime is here,
They dust me down and tell me
To show a little cheer.
Between the plaster snowman
And little glassy lake
They stand me in the middle
Of some ice-covered cake,
And for a while there's laughter,
But as the week wears on,
They cut up all the landscape
Till every scrap is gone.
Then with the plaster snowman
And little lake of glass
I'm banished to the cupboard
For one more year to pass.

LAST WISHES

When I'm ninety-one or -two,
Here's what I would have you do:
Let me by the chimney be,
With my dog for company,
Let me choose the food I eat,
Be it plain or be it sweet,
Let me wear my watch although
It may be an hour slow,
Let me play my tunes upon
My ancient accordion,
And let me have this book to read
Should I ever feel the need.

First published in the United States 1987 by
Dial Books for Young Readers
2 Park Avenue
New York, New York 10016

Published in Great Britain by
Hutchinson Children's Books Ltd.
Text copyright © 1987 by Colin West
Pictures copyright © 1987 by Julie Banyard
All rights reserved
Printed and bound in Great Britain
First edition
OBE
1 3 5 7 9 10 8 6 4 2

Library of Congress Cataloging in Publication Data
West, Colin. A moment in rhyme.
Summary: An illustrated collection of twenty-four poems
on a variety of subjects and experiences.
1. Children's poetry, English. [1. English poetry.]
I. Banyard, Julie, ill. II. Title.
PR6073.E763M64 1987 821'.914 86-24287
ISBN 0-8037-0259-0